Collection of Poetry

by

Matthew Stewart

RoseDog❧Books
PITTSBURGH, PENNSYLVANIA 15222

The contents of this work including, but not limited to, the accuracy of events, people, and places depicted; opinions expressed; permission to use previously published materials included; and any advice given or actions advocated are solely the responsibility of the author, who assumes all liability for said work and indemnifies the publisher against any claims stemming from publication of the work.

All Rights Reserved
Copyright © 2013 by Matthew Stewart

No part of this book may be reproduced or transmitted, downloaded, distributed, reverse engineered, or stored in or introduced into any information storage and retrieval system, in any form or by any means, including photocopying and recording, whether electronic or mechanical, now known or hereinafter invented without permission in writing from the publisher.

RoseDog Books
701 Smithfield Street
Pittsburgh, PA 15222
Visit our website at *www.rosedogbookstore.com*

ISBN: 978-1-4809-0014-1
eISBN: 978-1-4349-3448-2

Duluth

(Indian Bingo)
You can call it an activity;
you can give it any name
But when you stand to win or lose
it's more than just a game
You can say it's for the Indians,
as if you really care
The people down at City Hall,
they only want their share
You can speak of all the benefits
for the City of Duluth
But it's nothing more than gambling,
and you know that's the truth

Duluth

Life in Duluth is slowing down
People there are leaving town
Seeking jobs without success
The economy is such a mess
The mayor sits at City Hall
I wonder if he cares at all
People turning to life of crime
Policemen working overtime
Chasing those who steal and rob
But they thank the lord
They have a job

Home is where the Heart is

Home is where the heart is—
And I finally know the truth
No matter where I choose to go
My heart stays in Duluth
Florida has the beaches
And the sun it always shines
But I rather be in Minnesota
Among the Norwegian pines
California to has beaches
And all the movie stars
They drive up and down the avenues
In their fancy cars
But the things most important
For me are in Duluth
That is where my friends are
Yes I finally know the truth

I want to hold you in my arms

And taste the sweetness of your lips

As the passion rises between us

With the writhing of our hips

I want to taste the sweet nectar

That all of this has brung

As I drive you simply wild child!

With the slithering of my tongue

I am excited by your youthfulness,

yet you seem to be so wise

I would love to bury more than just

my head between your thighs

For me it's been quite some time,

but a soldier never dies

Please Forgive Me Mom

Please forgive me for all
the tears you ever wept
The nights you waited up
and when you never slept
For all the bad I've ever done, when
I lied and stole from everyone
When I denied you ever loved
your son – Please forgive me
For all the time I'd pretend to change,
I'd pretend to change yet stayed the same
For all the Love I tried to hide
But most of all, not there
with you when you died
Please forgive me

Ray Of Sunshine

A golden ray of sunshine
On a cloudy day
A pretty little flower
The sunrise on the bay
The pretty little flower
Is what you are to me
The golden ray of sunshine
Is what you'll always be
The sunrise on the bay
Is what I hope that we can share
I know it would be more beautiful
If only you were there

Gossip

They say believe
Half of what you see
None of what you hear
For nothing is as it seems
It hardly crystal clear
Some people live to gossip
I guess it is their choice
But personally, I believe
Their just in Love
With the sound
Of their own voice

Judgment

It's been said
People who just don't matter
People who matter don't judge
Well if that in itself
Is not a judgment
Then a judgment
There never was

Dear Lord

Dear Lord I Thank Thee
For my food
For my life and all that's good
For Jesus Christ
Your only son
Who died for me
And everyone

On Gifts

Sometime given on request
But seldom on demand

When you spoke and
the silence broke,
Something in my mind awoke.
Feelings I've promised to shun,
Can no longer easily be done.
The pain from the past
I promised would last,
Is fading as quickly as if
a spell had been cast.
Tho' I promised I would never
fall in love again,
I'm beginning to think of
you as more than a friend.

Feelings

Other quick to criticize
Fill our minds so full of lies
Secret doubts and silent fears
Come and go thru out the years
Sometimes brought out in times of stress
By people we feel we must impress
If you feel that's what you have to do
Then others will get the best of you
You're a very special person
Your feelings are special too
So learn to understand them better
And others soon will too

Younger Girl

I love the way you smile,
yet I hate the way you laugh
If we were together,
well you can do the math
You are so very sexy
and beautiful it's true
I would certainly do your mother
if she were anything like you.

Seabee's

A Seabee is a man full of
courage skill and pride
Ready to fight for freedom,
for which so many
Others died A man of
the Navy, a man of skill
Trained to build and trained to kill
They build our bases in far away places
Their men of the world and familiar faces
From Naples Italy to Rota Spain
From the Philippine Islands
To the desert plain
Respect these people as they do you
Their fighting Seabees and
They can do

Spring

Winters over, spring is here
Full of sunshine, love and cheer
The birds sing and the bees buzz
Make me think there never was a winter at all

Summer

Summer fun and summer sun
Doing things I've never done
A swimming pool, a sandy beach
And the whole world
Is within my reach
My mother was right
When she said to me
The finest things in
Life are free

Don't apologize

Just show it

For I've heard it all before

You sound sincere

But forgive me dear

I don't believe you anymore

Pipeline

Unfamiliar faces, it's always the same
Before the job is over you wil
know them by name
Working and working and
walking the line
It's a fine line the difference
between making a living and
losing your mind
Searching and searching, hoping to find
Peace, serenity and soundness of mind
With constant thoughts of
those they left behind
Some seek comfort in the
arms of strangers embraces
It eases the pain but it never replaces
The love of a family and
their smiling faces
Long days, even longer nights
Petty squabbles and senseless fights
But for this challenge we unite
To get it done and do it right

Soon the line will be completed
only soon to be repeated
Then it's time to pickup to
packup, time to move on
This one's but a memory,
For the money's now all gone

Someday

Someday I want to travel
In elegance and style
Relaxing and enjoying
Each and every mile
But until I find the silver lining
In the clouds that follow me
I will have to travel however I can
And see the sights for free
The mountains and the valleys
The hills and the streams
They will have to do for now
But won't satisfy my dreams

NATURE

When you wake up in the morning
And the air is fresh and clear
And Nature is calling to you
yet no one seems to hear
As you walk to the factory that
discharges smog into the air
And you read about conservation
and say it isn't fair
'Cuz you're worried about the jobs
And the price you'd have to pay
To see it all start changing
and turn the other way
You just want to make a living
And send all your kids to school
The lake might get polluted
But we'll have a swimming pool.

Me, You and Baseball

I will always be your number one fan
You don't have to get a big hit
to score With me.
A swing and a miss is
when I swing By and your not
there and I miss you
You don't have to worry about
striking Out with me
We don't have to have a board to
Know the score
It doesn't matter whether it's day
Or night we can always
make a Game
We don't need a uniform to
know Your on my team
You're my star in the hall of fame
You're my franchise player and
I would Never trade you
You love baseball and I love you

Dad

His life was never easy but never
once did he complain
He felt it served no purpose
that it only was in vain
He lost his mother very young
and he grew up very fast
I know his life was colorful
although I never asked
He never dressed real fancy
he was of the working class
And if you didn't like it,
well, you could surely kiss his ass
He loved to plant his flowers
And the other things he did
There was an excitement
when he spoke of them,
just like a little kid
When he knew his time was coming
His thoughts were of others still
He was worried
how they might take it,

and the pain that they might feel
Forsake not his memory
with pity or remorse
For he's gone to a better place
and life has run its course

Black bear on the Lakewalk

I have something in common
With that big black bear
I once enjoyed the solitude and serenity
Of going down there
Now the sightseers and tourists
They tremble with fear
When they stumble across me
As I sit by the fire enjoying a beer
Then they point and they stare
And say whats he doing there
Then they quicken their pace
And flee in despair
Yes I have something in common
With that big black bear

Walls

I built my walls,
brick by brick
I built them tall and o' so thick
And if they were to fall,
you would find
That just behind there
was just another wall
On superficial subjects,
I can ramble on with ease
I can talk about the good times or
anything you please
But ask me about my feelings or
how I deal with shame
Well go ahead and deal the cards,
let's play another game
I built my walls, I knew I must
The world outside I did not trust
And now I am surrounded
with my doubts and fears
Those throughout the years
are totally unfounded

The little drummer boy

When I think of Christmas
I don't think of a toy
I remember the story
Of the little drummer boy
He came to the manger, with nothing
But the clothes he had worn
But he wanted to be there
When Jesus was born
There came wise men with gifts
Of silver and gold
Others from afar with riches untold
The little drummer boy had
nothing to give
That you could carry along
So he gave of himself
For he gave him his song
That's where the spirit of Christmas
Received its first start
The little drummer boy who
had nothing to give
But the love in his heart

Family

My family means to me
What sunshine means to a growing tree
They love me and show they care
And let me know they'll always be there
My father is a very proud man
Going thru life doing the best he can
He wants us to have what he never had
He's loving and understanding, yes that's my dad
My mother is such a beautiful woman
In so many different ways
She always put her family first
Every night when she kneels and prays
My brothers are my closest friends
That I could ever know
Together we climbed the hills and
Fished the streams
We lived our lives and shared our dreams
My sister too, are my closest friends
That I could ever know
Never would I think to trade them
For a diamond, a jewel

Or the finest jade

Yes when God passed out Families

I must have been first in Line

How other could I have got

A family as fine a mine

Life

Life is what you want it to be
Life for me is living free
Taking chances on short romances
Having fun and going to dances
Life is loving people and being loved
Life is being open and honest
with others And yourself
Not hiding your problems away on a shelf
I love life and I love me
I want to live I want to be
I want to see what others see
And figure out what's best for me
I want to be a friend to people
And help them on their way
I don't want to live in tomorrow
Just take things day by day
These are the things I want for me
These are the things I want to be
It may take a while but wait and see
I'll be living a life, content and free
Living the life that was meant for me

Three little kittens

I have three little kittens
With little white mittens
And all they do is play
All the live long day
They run and leap
And play hide and seek
And the rest of the time
They like to eat
And crawl up on the bed to sleep
Oh little kittens I love you so
It's so much fun
To watch you grow

Recovery

To all the people that I met
To all the ones I won't forget
To all the ones that bared their soul
To all the ones that lost control
Recovery's a lifelong process
We have all suffered many losses
Now its time to abstain
To live our lives and feel the pain
May you find that inner child
that lies within us all
You know your only killing it
With drugs & alcohol
No one says its easy for
the path is often rough
But the burden is much easier
If you dealing with your stuff
You know the stuff that's deep inside you
The anger guilt & shame
You know the stuff your hiding
That's driving you insane
May you find that higher power

Whatever it may be
It's the only way you'll find yourself
Restored to sanity

AA

I used to be an actor, successful to some degree
I acted happy all the time, as if nothing bothered me
No costume was ever needed, for I wore a superficial mask
I spent much time to have the answers,
to the questions one Might ask
I could anticipate the questions
So I very seldom spoke
Then one night suddenly, as if by magic
This inner self awoke
No longer did I need to ponder,
the words that I had Spoken
I was confident that this was me
And not just what I was smoking
The crystallized illusions,
the memories haunt me still
But at least I realize
I have not the answers
And perhaps I never will
Thru my arrogant delusions where
I thought I found control
I lost a lot of friends I knew

And almost lost my soul
Sometimes when I'm feeling down
And I'm yearning for that high
I remind myself that if I go back
That surely I will die
But sometimes it doesn't matter
Knowing the prince I'd pay
Those are the times that I'm most
Thankful
For the people in AA/NA

The Tragic Clown

With the performance he gives
You can't help but grin
It opens the door but
he won't let you in
His rambling thoughts,
they seem so obscure
But if you listen real close,
well then I'm no so sure
If you could hear
what he's not saying,
perhaps you'd understand
The life that he's living,
is not what he planned
He turns to the needle
to deaden the pain
It works pretty well but
it drives him insane
He's headed for prison
and he rather die
But nothing so much matters,
so long as he's high

The tragic clown

Someone everybody loves

But no one understands

Another Day

Another day, another dollar
Another drink, another binge
Another day of being that way
Is like having a job that doesn't pay
Another toke, another smoke
And life becomes a senseless joke
Another high just getting by
Again I'm living a losers lie
A day just past and the high don't last
Better get another one,
and better get it fast
I'm going to stop, I'm going to try
Theres more to life than getting high
But who will help me along the way
My friends are drunk and wasting away
They come down to celebrate
But not to help a friend go straight
The bottle that brought me sorrow
The bottle that caused me pain
The bottle that is my enemy
To think I once thought it

A friend

I never fit in, I had to fight

They teased me and beat me

What gave them the right?

My mom was very ill

Her health would slowly fail

I prayed to God to help her

But it was all to no avail

I stole her medications

Cause I couldn't take the pain

The guilt and shame of what I've done

Is driving me insane

I drank for confidence
and now I have none,
Now I drink to escape
the things I have done.
I drank to be accepted
as part of the clan,
To silence the fears
I had as a man.
I drank for reasons
I couldn't explain,
I drank to find happiness
but only found pain.

The Day Is Coming

The day is coming
I know it's soon.
The music is changing,
to a different tune.
Like all high heads,
I'll pay the cost
I fought the battle and now I lost
It was dope that made me lose
The partying and all the booze
It's alright to party,
if that's where it ends,
But not too break entry
with a couple of friends,
To say I was drunk and
didn't know what I did
Is not only childish,
but typical of a kid.
I've used those lines several times
Sure drinking helps you do things,
you usually might not
But so many think it's alright

if I don't get caught.
They can say I've been here
and I've been there
They're picking on me,
it just isn't fair
But if you keep on getting into trouble
Who's picking on whom?
You don't get into trouble
For something you didn't do.

Knight

I'm a knight in tarnished armor
No castle to defend
No dragons have I ever slain
I've only made pretend
No maiden have I rescued
No damsels in distress
I've not done more
Than just get by
For this I must confess
For in my life theres
Many dragons
That surely must be slain
If I am ever to find my
Princess
And end this loneliness
And pain

Dear Self,

I am sorry I am so hard on you;
it's just that you can be such
an idiot at times. You can be so self-absorbed,
as you think the whole world revolves
around you. You can be such a pity monger.
If you read this letter a couple of months
from now, I hope it's at a time
that you know how it is to
interact with others without
fear of judgment or rejection.
I hope you have found acceptance
and friendship. I hope you have learned
to give to others that which
you hope for yourself.

Self

PSYCH WARD

Little rooms square and small
Nursing station down the hall
With little me trapped inside
Stropped of dignity and my pride
Little doctors with little black books
Walking, talking, staring and scaring
They're going to take you,
shake you and try to make you
Their ideas of a man
So think for yourself while you still can.

In life I feel alone

An isolation of my own making

Conceived by my own actions

Imposed by my own self will

How could I expect you to understand

One you live amongst the crowds

Thrives amongst the masses

One who's very existence

Demands never to ever

Be alone

2nd Step

I grew up with religion,
they told us we must pray
They told us we must do it
each and every day
They told us of an angry God,
they told us of damnation
They told us that man was born in sin
Ever since creation
So when it came to the second step
and I needed a Power greater
I decided I'd use the group for now
I'd settle with God later

Gratitude

I've been feeling down
and wondering why
And now I think I know
There sure has been little gratitude
In the feelings that I show
There's got to be some gratitude
Somewhere in my attitude
I must change my way of thinking
For if there is no gratitude in my attitude
Then soon I will be drinking

Twelve Steps

1) First step you must confess
   your powerless you lifes a mess

2) Second step is of belief that
   only God can bring relief

3) Third step – give your will and life
   to God above and God will fill your
   heart with love

4) A fearless moral search we make
   the hardest step we will have to take

5) Admit to God ourselves and another
   one the exact nature of what we've done

6) Were entirely read for him to remove
   our defects of characterso our lives
   will soon improve

7) Humbly now we request take our
   short comings leave the rest

8) We make a list of those we've
   harmed and why they're pissed

9) Make direct amends to those
   we have harmed not just our friends

10) A daily inventorys taken and
    we admit when were mistaken

11) Thru daily prayer and meditation
    God will improve our situation

12) Carry the message in all that
    you do for words are just that
    and your actions are true

NA

How did I do it
I don't really know
Cause you're the ones that,
have taught me
Helped me to grow
How did I do it
I can't really say
I made it an hour
Then I made it a day
How did I do it
Slowly at first
Working the steps
Never quenching my thirst
How did I do it
I haven't a clue
I don't have the answers
I get them from you

Carry the Message (12 Step)

Carry the message in
all that you do
For words are just that yet
your actions are true
Your family, your friends and
the changes they've seen
In the way that your living
now that your clean
This is the twelfth step
The most rewarding of all
That feeling you get when
you get the call
You need not preach it, promote it
For I have a notion
Your smile my friend is its
Greatest promotion

Don't preach it
Before you reach it

I am Looking for a Sponsor

I am looking for a sponsor,
the program it demands
I am looking for a sponsor,
one who understands
I am looking for a sponsor,
who's not arrogant or crass
Who doesn't think the program means,
I have to kiss his ass
I am looking for a sponsor,
whose program is much stronger
I know I'll never find one,
if this list gets too much longer

Treatment

He walked thru the door
With his eyes to the floor
Carrying his stuff in the bags
That he got from the store
They said can I help you please
He just trembled and shook
For he was definitely sure
That he knew that look
They looking him down
From his head to his toe
And he could decide
Whether to stay, or whether to go
However, a power greater than himself
Kept him in check
For he had lost everything he had
And his life was a wreck
They assigned him a group
After a couple of days
He was still somewhat shaky
And half in a daze
He looked around the room
Thinking why am I here
I don't drink liquor

I only drink beer

They said who might you be

And what brought you here now

He wanted to explain but didn't know how

He stuttered and stammered yet

He managed his name

Then he started talking in circles

And shifted the blame

They said if nothing ever changes

Then its always the same

Little by little he started to share

He listened to other and began to compare

Thinking I know what they mean

For I've certainly been there

After a couple of week passed

It had been quite a while

He started to open up and managed a smile

He started caring about others

That he hardly knew

And listened to them or what he might do

They said there five steps you will learn About

And seven more when you get out

The first step you must confess

Your powerless your lifes a mess

The second step is of belief
That only God can bring relief
The third step we give our will
And lives to God above
And God will fill our live with love
The forth step – a fearless moral
Search we take perhaps
The hardest step we will have to make
Then we admit to God, ourselves
And another one
The exact nature of what we've done
Now you have an idea of what
Its all about but remember
Theres seven more when you get Out
Find a sponsor and go to Meetings
For they will keep you on Track
For theres no guarantee
You will ever make it back

Wanting nothing

more than to wake up

With someone there beside me

Yet searching amid

a sea of souls that seldom sleep

I have auditioned for many roles

But I've yet to get the part

Perhaps because I was never

much good at acting

Much better at reacting

So I guess that makes me a reactor

Not nuclear, but certainly explosive